The National Parks

Through Our Eyes

Deirdre K. Fuller & Robert C. Fuller

Other books by Deirdre and Robert Fuller
- Waffle's Trip to Big Bend National Park
- To the Miss I Really Miss
- Pugs in the Park

Arches National Park
Utah

Assateague National Seashore
Maryland, Virginia

Big Bend National Park
Texas

Blue Ridge Parkway
North Carolina, Virginia

Canyonlands
Utah

Grand Canyon National Park
South Rim
Arizona

Grand Canyon National Park
North Rim
Arizona

Grand Teton National Park
Wyoming

Laguna Atascosa National Wildlife Refuge

Texas

Little Bighorn Battlefield National Monument
Montana

Little River Canyon National Preserve
Alabama

Mount Rushmore National Memorial
South Dakota

Russell Cave National Monument

Alabama

Yellowstone National Park
Idaho, Montana, Wyoming